DINOSAUR
DOT-TO-DOTS

JO MOON

ARCTURUS

This edition published in 2018 by Arcturus Publishing Limited
26/27 Bickels Yard, 151–153 Bermondsey Street,
London SE1 3HA

Edited by JMS Books llp with Sebastian Rydberg
Layout by Chris Bell
Illustrations by Jo Moon

ISBN: 978-1-78828-502-5
CH005804NT
Supplier 29, Date 0118, Print run 6202

Printed in China

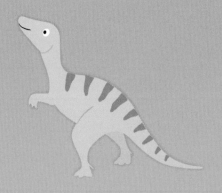

Early Dinosaur

This dinosaur looked like a bird.
It had long legs and a wishbone.

Coelophysis (see-loh-FISE-iss) was one of the first dinosaurs and was good at running.

Land of the Dinosaurs

A plant-eater and a meat-eater are out for lunch. Find out what they look like.

As big as a bus, Stegosaurus (STEG-oh-SORE-us) had lots of bony plates on its back.

Tyrannosaurus rex
(ty-RAN-oh-SORE-us)
had 50 huge teeth.

5

Fierce Meat-Eaters

These creatures lived around 280 million years ago. Discover what they are up to.

This pair of Dimetrodon (dy-MET-roh-don) are ready for a fight!

Twice as long as a horse, they had large sails on their backs.

Tyrant King

Both of these dinosaurs ran on two feet.
Find out which one is the biggest!

Little Compsognathus
(comp-sog-NAY-thus)
was the size of a chicken.

T. rex weighed nine tons and had teeth as big as bananas.

Taller Than a House

Connect the dots to see which tall creature is lunching like a giraffe!

The giant Brachiosaurus (BRAH-kee-oh-SORE-us) lived in large family groups.

It used its very long
neck to feed on leaves
at the tops of trees.

11

Dinosaur Battle

Discover which dinosaurs are
fighting in the desert.

The speedy Velociraptor (veh-LOSS-ee-rap-tuhr) was covered in feathers.

Plant-eating Protoceratops (PRO-toh-SEH-rah-tops) was about the size of a cow.

13

Headbangers!

See how these bone-headed dinosaurs did battle with each other using their bumpy heads.

Pachycephalosaurus (pak-ee-SEF-uh-lo-SORE-us) rammed their heads together when they fought.

Their skulls were about 30 times thicker than a human's.

Whip Tails

Discover one of the longest land animals that ever lived on Earth.

It laid small clutches of eggs in nests, which took up to 82 days to hatch.

76 75 74 73
77 72
78 71 70
79
66 67 69 68
80 63
92 64 65
1 94 62
2 93
81 91
3 85 90
4 86
82 89
84 7
83 87 88
5 6 13 14
12 11 15
8 9 10

55 54
56
53
57 47 45
52 50 48
60 58 59 51
61
21 49 32
20 22
19
29 28
23
24 26
17 25 16

40 39 38
41 37
36
46 44 42
34
43 35
33
31 30
27

The very long tail of the Diplodocus (dip-LOH-doh-kus) had about 80 bones in it.

Crest Head

Connect the dots to see some unusual dinosaurs feeding on plants.

Parasaurolophus (PA-ra-sore-OL-off-us) used its bony head crest for trumpeting.

Duck-billed Hadrosaurus (HAD-ro-sore-us) weighed as much as an elephant.

Giant Skull!

It's time to meet one of the largest horned dinosaurs ever. It only ate plants!

Torosaurus (TOR-oh-SORE-us) was a herbivore that lived near the sea in North America.

It had one of the biggest skulls of any land animal and a big neck frill.

21

Feeding Time

Connect the dots to find out what these dinosaurs have in common.

Stegosaurus (STEG-oh-SORE-us) had large, bony plates and a tiny brain.

Ceratasaurus (keh-RAT-oh-SORE-us) had short front legs and a horn on its nose.

23

The Chase Is On!

Discover which relative of the Tyrannosaurus is on the hunt!

Ostrich-like Gallimimus (gal-ih-MY-mus) ran twice as fast as an Olympic sprinter!

With its big, strong jaws, Tarbosaurus (TAR-boh-SORE-us) was a great hunter.

Spiny Lizard

Which huge dinosaur, bigger than T. rex, is fishing for lunch?

Spinosaurus (SPINE-oh-SORE-us) had an amazing sail on its back.

It was one of the largest meat-eating dinosaurs ever to have walked the Earth.

Tusk, Tusk!

Discover what these dinosaurs are getting their teeth into today.

Heterodontosaurus (HET-er-oh-DONT-oh-SORE-us) had three kinds of teeth, including tusks.

Massospondylus (mas-oh-SPON-di-lus) walked on two legs and ate mostly plants.

Fighting Machines

Who do you think would win in the battle between these two fierce dinosaurs?

Ankylosaurus (AN-kih-loh-SORE-us) had huge, bony plates to protect against attackers.

It used its heavy club tail as a weapon in fights with dinosaurs such as T. rex.

31

Good Mother

These baby dinosaurs will grow very quickly to be as big and strong as their parents.

Pack Hunters

Some dinosaurs liked to hunt in groups.
Find out which ones are on the move today.

Deinonychus (dy-NON-ik-us) had large, hooked claws on its back legs.

Apatosaurus (ah-PAT-oh-SORE-us) had a long, flexible neck and ate plants.

Big Chicken!

Meet the dinosaur that was covered with feathers and hatched its eggs like a chicken.

Oviraptor (OH-vee-RAP-tor) had a powerful parrotlike beak and no teeth.

Scientists think that it used its beak to crack eggs or break open shellfish.

Fishing Dinosaurs

Discover a fish-eating dinosaur that had a long jaw and nose, just like a crocodile.

Crocodiles are ancient creatures that have lived on Earth for over 200 million years.

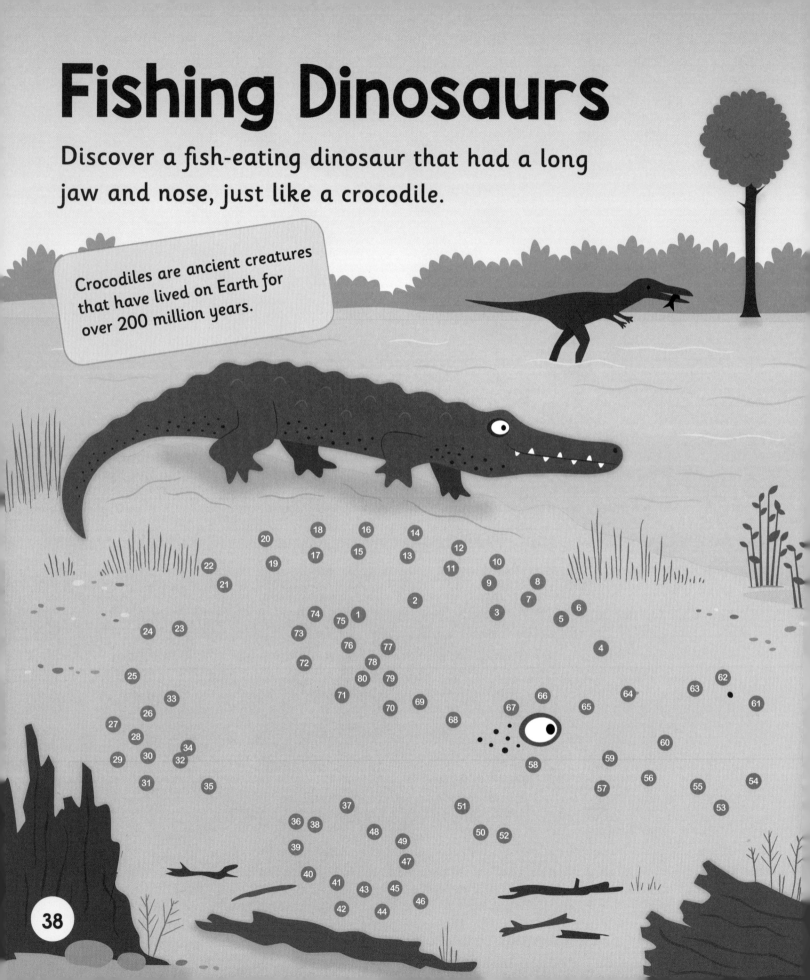

Baryonyx (BAH-ree-ON-icks) lived near rivers and used its large claws to hunt fish.

Bright Head

These dinosaurs liked to move around in small groups. Find out what they looked like.

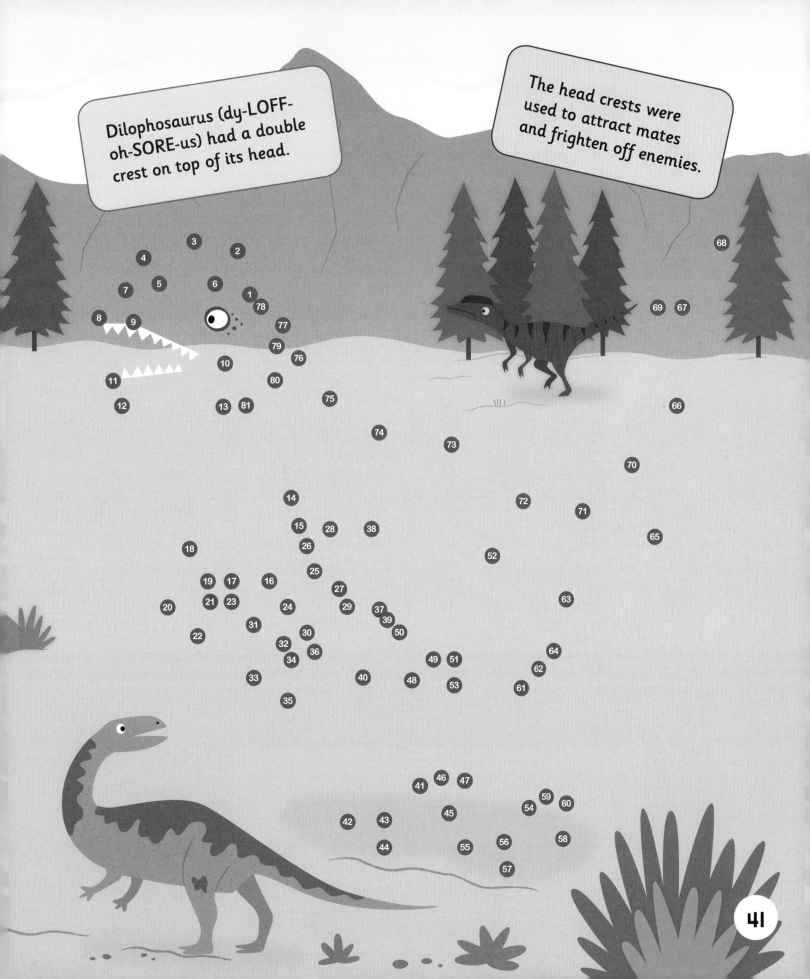

Dilophosaurus (dy-LOFF-oh-SORE-us) had a double crest on top of its head.

The head crests were used to attract mates and frighten off enemies.

41

Three-Horned Beast

T. rex is on the prowl today. Find out which dinosaur it has its eye on.

Triceratops (try-SEH-ra-tops) had three horns, a large neck frill, and a parrotlike beak.

It needed its three horns to fight off T. rex and to protect its young.

43

Dinosaurs and Birds

Discover two dinosaurs that looked like the birds we see today!

Protarchaeopteryx (PRO-tark-ee-OPT-er-ix) had feathers but could not fly.

Archaeopteryx (ARK-ee-OPT-er-ix) had wings and could glide from treetops.

Thumbs Up!

It's time to meet a dinosaur that ate only plants but was as big as an elephant.

Iguanodon (ig-WAH-noh-don) weighed as much as two small cars and had a ducklike beak.

It used a sharp spike on its thumb to attack its enemies.

47

Lions of the Jurassic

Connect the dots to find out which dinosaur used to hunt in packs, like lions.

Allosaurus (AL-oh-SORE-us) had a pair of horns, strong claws, and knifelike teeth.

It hunted creatures bigger than itself, such as the plant-eating Diplodocus (dip-LOH-doh-kus).

Meat-Eating Giant

This huge dinosaur lived millions of years earlier than T. rex. Find out what it looked like.

Giganotosaurus (jig-an-OH-toe-SORE-us) was taller and longer but slimmer than T. rex.

It had a very small brain and three fingers on each hand, not two like T.rex.

51

Night Hunters

See which clever dinosaur with big eyes is able to hunt in the dark.

Troodon (TROH-oh-don) had front-facing eyes that helped it to see prey at night.

It had a large brain for its small size and was one of the smartest dinosaurs.

53

Giant Predators

This close relative of T. rex is coming face-to-face with a fierce, river-dwelling reptile!

Deinosuchus (dy-no-SOO-kus) was five times bigger and heavier than alligators today.

Albertosaurus (al-BERT-oh-SORE-us) weighed as much as an average family car.

88

25
23   27
24   26
22
21   28
20

17   15   13
19   14   1   12
16   4   2   29
18   6   3   11
8   7   5
9   10
96
93   95
92   94
30

90
91

31
67   32
33
86   46   39
40   38   34
83   66   47   45   41   36
85   68   43
84   63   37   35
65   48   44   42
64
82
81   62   49
69
71   70   61
80   79   60
78   50
77   72   59
76
74   51
75   57
73   58
55   53
56   54   52

55

Biggest Dinosaur

Connect the dots and be amazed by the heaviest and longest land animal ever!

Argentinosaurus (AR-juhn-TEE-no-SORE-us) may have weighed as much as 14 African elephants.

With its neck lifted up, it was as tall as a building with seven floors!

57

Duck-Billed Dinos

This noisy dinosaur lived in herds.
Find out what it looked like.

Saurolophus (SORE-oh-LOAF-us) had a spike-shaped crest on its head and a toothless beak.

It used the crest to call other dinosaurs in the herd and warn them of danger.

Flying Reptiles

These prehistoric fliers had sharp teeth, wings, and four grabbing claws!

Pterosaurs (TEH-roh-sores) were the first animals to fly, after insects.

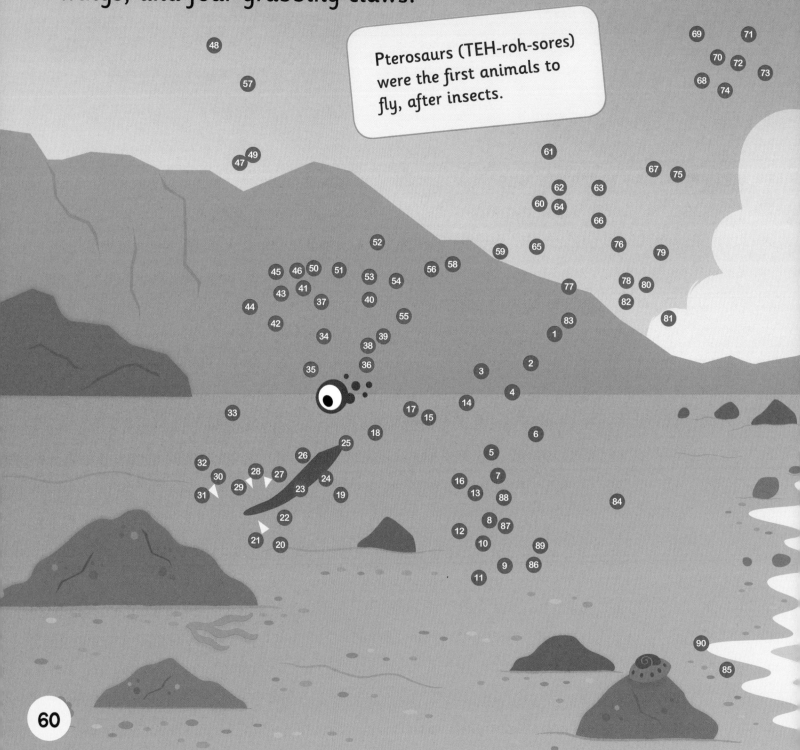

When Dimorphodon (dy-MOR-foh-don) landed, it used its wings to walk.

Winged Terrors!

The name of the best-known pterosaur means "winged finger."

Pterodactylus (TEH-ro-DACK-tih-lus) was the first pterosaur ever discovered.

Its wing was made of skin stretching behind a long finger bone.

Beaky!

Meet another high-flying dinosaur with an unusually shaped head.

Dsungaripterus (SUN-ga-RIP-ter-us) had a long, sharp beak like a pair of tweezers.

It used its pointed beak to remove shellfish from cracks in rocks.

65

Long Wings

Now you can see what the largest flying animal of all time looked like!

Quetzalcoatlus (KWETS-ul-koh-AT-luss) had the wingspan of a small plane.

It flew long distances and swooped down on its prey.

67

Monsters of the Deep

Look at these large, swimming reptiles with long, snakelike necks!

Plesiosaurs (PLEH-zee-oh-SORES) used their paddle-shaped flippers to swim.

They swung their necks from side to side to catch their food.

Snaky Beast!

Wonder at this strange creature that swam thousands of miles using its four flippers.

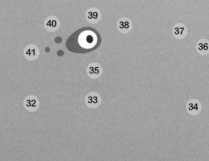
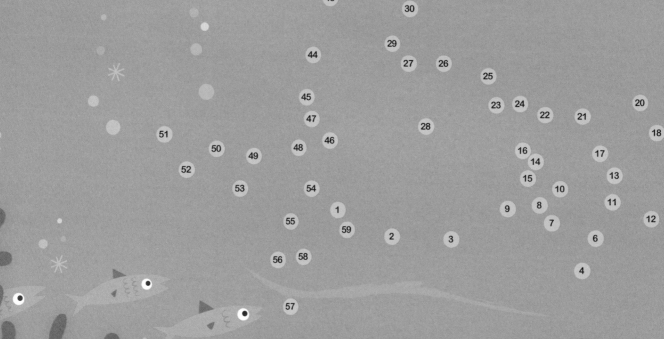
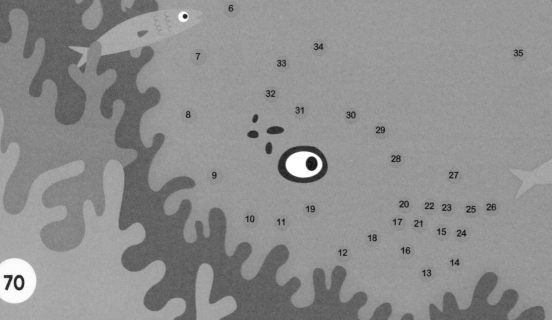

Elasmosaurus (el-LAZZ-moh-SORE-us) had an extremely long neck.

Its bendy neck helped it to suddenly snap at its prey.

71

Terrible Crocodiles

Find out more about the very long and very scary cousin of modern alligators.

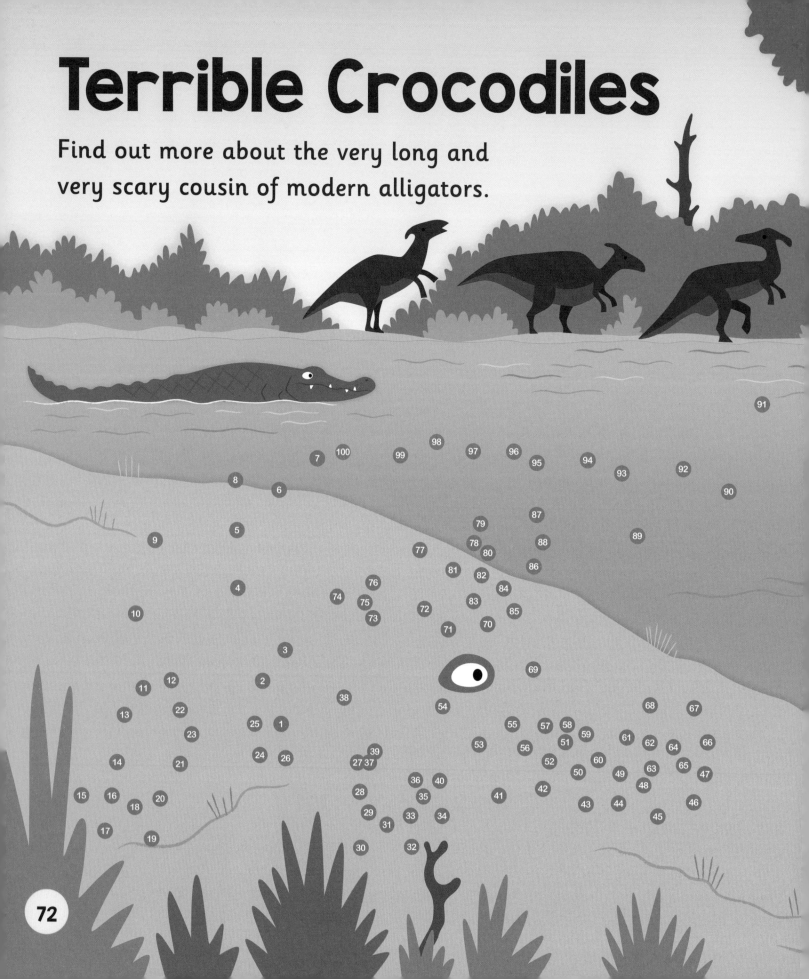

Giant Sharks

The ancient sea was full of huge, strange fish. Here are some unusual sharks!

Megalodon (meh-GAH-lo-don) was one of the largest, most powerful fish ever.

Helicoprion (heh-lih-KO-pree-on) had a sawlike spiral of 180 teeth.

Big Eyes

Get ready to see some marine reptiles that lived like dolphins.

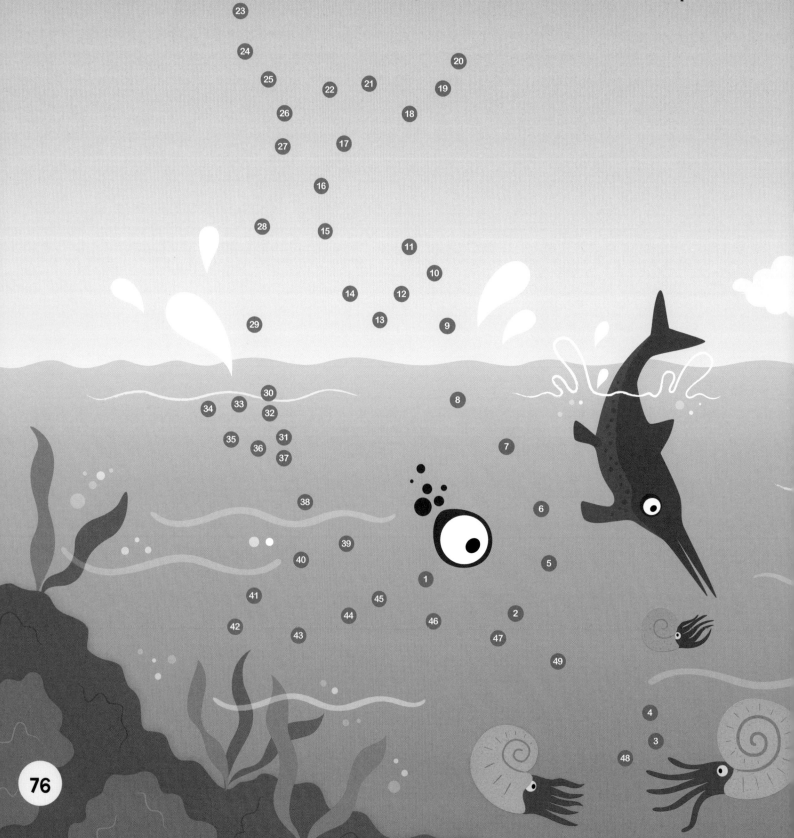

Ichthyosaurus (ICK-thee-oh-SORE-us) had dozens of very sharp teeth.

It used its huge eyes to hunt for ammonites and other crunchy prey.

Huge Jaws!

Prepare to meet one of the most feared sea monsters ever!

Liopleurodon (LY-oh-PLOO-ro-don) had huge and powerful jaws.

It had big teeth, shaped like spikes, and a bite stronger than T. rex's.

Mighty Lizards

Discover what this enormous underwater hunter looked like, if you dare!

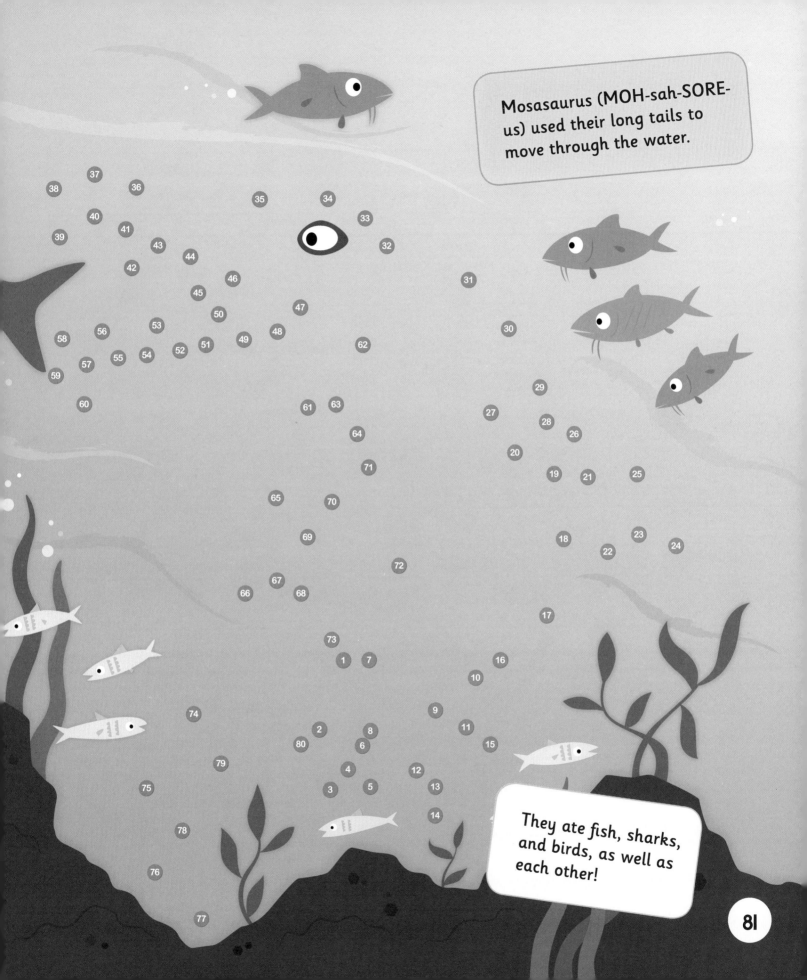

Mosasaurus (MOH-sah-SORE-us) used their long tails to move through the water.

They ate fish, sharks, and birds, as well as each other!

81

End of the Dinosaurs

Connect the dots to see what
life on Earth was like
before a huge asteroid hit.

The big space rock wiped out all the dinosaurs around 66 million years ago.

Pterosaurs and many of the giant sea reptiles also disappeared.

83

After the Dinosaurs

Find out which scary animals lived on Earth after the dinosaurs.

Smilodon (SMY-lo-don) was a cat with very long, sharp teeth.

Megatherium (meg-ah-THEER-ee-em) was a giant ground sloth.

40 41
42
39 29 43
38 44
37 45
36 35 30
34 28
33 32 31 27 46
1
26 47
14
20 22 25 48
24 12 2 49
15
19 21 23 3
13
16 72
18 50
17
10 51
8 60
11 4 74
9 75
7
6 5 73
71
76
59
61
70
77 86 53
62 58
85
78 69
79 52
83 84
80 68 64 63 54
67 57
81 82 66 65 55
56

Dig It Up!

Meet the people who dig up dinosaur bones from millions of years ago.

Scientists study the fossils to learn about what the dinosaurs looked like.

They use dynamite, drills, picks, and even toothbrushes during a dig.

87

In the Museum

Connect the dots to see what
enormous creature is on show here.

Solutions

On the following pages, we show you what was hidden in the pictures. Once you have connected the dots, your drawings should look just like these.

Page 3

Pages 4-5

Pages 6-7

Pages 8-9

Pages 10-11

Pages 12-13

Pages 14-15

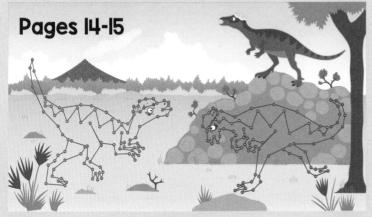

Pages 16-17

Pages 18-19

Pages 20-21

Pages 22-23

Pages 24-25

Pages 26-27

Pages 28-29

Pages 30-31

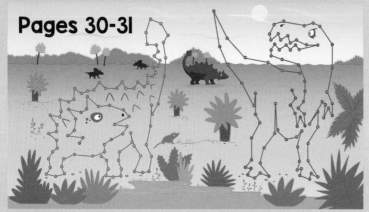

Pages 32-33

Pages 34-35

Pages 36-37

Pages 38-39

Pages 40-41

Pages 42-43

Pages 44-45

Pages 46-47

Pages 48-49

Pages 50-51

Pages 52-53

Pages 54-55

Pages 56-57

Pages 58-59

Pages 60-61

Pages 62-63

Pages 64-65

Pages 66-67

Pages 68-69

Pages 70-71

Pages 72-73

Pages 74-75

Pages 76-77

Pages 78-79

Pages 80-81

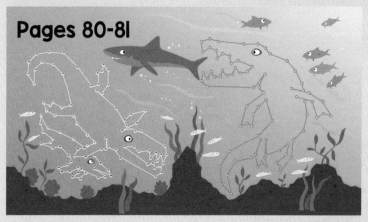

Pages 82-83

Pages 84-85

Pages 86-87

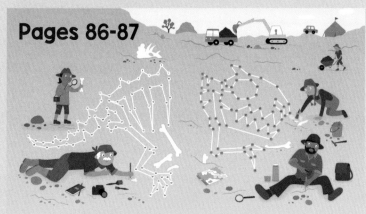

Pages 88-89